D0358838

Colour Right
Dress Right

The Total Look

Colour

Right Dress Right

The Total Look
Liz E. London and Anne H. Adams

Dorling Kindersley·London

Contents

Importance of colour

Colour is important; it affects how we feel and how people respond to us. Industries use stimulating colours to increase production, hospitals use soothing colours to enhance recuperation, advertisers employ eye-catching colours to entice us to buy their products.

Researchers have found that colours evoke certain responses. For instance, navy blue suggests authority. Red is exciting, stimulating; pink, sweet and gentle; orange is friendly, outgoing; yellow, sunny and cheerful. Green makes us feel tranquil and blue is also a soothing colour. Purple is regal, dignified; brown, dependable; black is sophisticated and mysterious; white is innocent and grey is safe, comforting and protective.

So colours are important in creating the look we want to achieve and influencing other people's mental reactions to us. A navy suit teamed with a white shirt is especially authoritative and commands respect. Neutral colours (such as black, grey, taupe, beige and cream) in various shades of the same tone create an elegant look; contrasting light and dark colours create a dramatic effect. Of course, a colour can also have negative associations. For example, too much pink can be saccharine.

Obviously, not everyone responds to colour in exactly the same way, but general responses are so well proved that they can be relied upon. According to John T. Molloy, author of *Dress for Success*, men are attracted to women wearing pale yellow, pale pink, navy, shades of blue, red and tan. They do not like mustard, chartreuse or lavender shades.

Women are instinctively attracted to the colours that most become them, but, unfortunately, they do not always select their most flattering colours because of the influence of parents, friends, sales people and childhood associations with colour.

Women are also influenced by colours and styles currently in vogue. Each season designers show their new ranges in particular colours, and fashion-conscious women are the first to wear them. But the latest colours may not always be the right ones for every woman. The right shades are those that accentuate the natural hair, skin, and eye colouring.

In recent years the Chinese and Japanese influence on fashion has resulted in a new simplicity – a rethinking of colour and design. They use neutrals as important basic colours.

Colour is the most important element in either enhancing your appearance or detracting from it. The easiest way to look your most attractive is to wear your best colours. If someone compliments you on the way you look, it probably means that the colour you have chosen is right for you.

Brunettes

Hair colour:
Medium-to-dark brown, black or jet-black

Complexion:
White-beige, beige with a hint of pink, golden beige (Oriental skin tones), or light or dark olive

Eye colour:
Brown, hazel, speckled tones of grey or green, grey or deep blue

Rows of bright red poppies, clusters of white orchids, and sprigs of violets provide you with the right background.

Your best colours are from the palette of the artist Mondrian: black, white, red and blue.

Cool colours are the colours for you – those that have blue undertones, such as deep red, green, and blue-green. Pure white is especially flattering against your dark hair colour, as are the white-based tones of frosty pink, blue, mint and lemon.

Clear and vivid colours make you look outstanding. You can wear combinations of sharply contrasting colours such as black and white, red and white and red and black as well as blue and black, navy and burgundy and orchid and green.

Warm colours, colours that have yellow or gold added, are to be avoided: gold, orange, ginger, brown, red with a yellow cast, green with a yellow cast and rust. Soft pastels, also, are not flattering for you.

● Brunettes with olive skin look particularly attractive in white, navy or magenta.

● Fair skins appear more vivacious in bright shades of emerald, purple and red. Off-white is preferable to pure white as this can be harsh against very fair skin.

● Oriental skins glow in magenta, purple and poppy red.

Altered hair colour

True brunettes never look their best as blondes. Nevertheless, should you decide to dye your hair blonde, make sure that the colour is in ash tones. Never use warm, red or golden tones. The same is true of highlights – ash tones will give a much lighter look and flatter your complexion.

Jet-black hair is the most flattering for Oriental skin tones and colouring your hair red or blonde is not recommended.

Brunettes tend to grey prematurely, and the grey usually becomes a clear silver white. Grey hair can be left natural, or highlighted with a rinse. If you wish to cover the grey, dye it a shade or two lighter than your original hair colour.

Brunette types

Brown-black hair
Pinky-beige complexion
Blue eyes

Jet-black hair
White-beige complexion
Hazel eyes

Silver-grey hair
Beige complexion
Grey-blue eyes

Medium-brown hair
Light olive complexion
Brown eyes

Your colour chart

The 24 colours below were selected especially for brunettes who look stunning in cool, blue-based tones. The first ten colours are your core colours. Any one of these is appropriate for all the basic items in your wardrobe – coats, suits, skirts and trousers. The neutral shades are also the most suitable for accessories. The remaining colours are more adaptable as accent colours for smaller items such as sweaters, blouses and scarves.

On the following pages we recommend shades of these colours for choosing cosmetics, accessories and jewellery, and we suggest wardrobe colour combinations on p. 72.

You can carry your colours everywhere by taking your colour chart to use as a shopping guide.

Your core colours

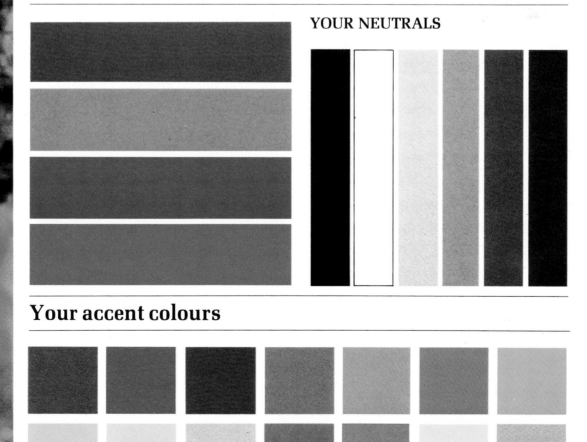

YOUR NEUTRALS

Your accent colours

Your best colours

Below are the right colours for your cosmetics and accessories. They reflect the colours we have set down for you on the previous page. Always think about the three or four colours in your wardrobe (see p. 72) and choose the "extras" to match them. When you go shopping, take along your colour chart to help you choose a neutral handbag or a bright lipstick that will co-ordinate with your clothes. You will soon achieve a total look in which everything – clothes, cosmetics and accessories – works together.

COSMETICS

Foundation　Rose-beige, medium-beige, light beige, cocoa, rose-brown, dark bronze. Avoid any beiges with gold tones

Blusher　Blue-pink, rose-brown, rose-wine

Eye shadow　Plum, taupe, blue, grey, grey-green, mauve

Eye liner　Charcoal, taupe

Mascara　Brown-black, electric blue

Lipstick　Bright red, cherry red, pink-plum, bright burgundy, fuchsia

Lip pencil　Red, plum

Nail varnish　Bright red, plum, fuchsia

ACCESSORIES

Glasses　If you wear glasses, you can wear more eye colour. Pink and blue or purple eye shadow combinations accentuate blue eyes; green or blue shadow can be used for brown eyes. Good colours for frames are bur-gundy, grey, red or very dark tortoise-shell. Avoid gold, tan, camel and peach

Jewellery　Sapphire, garnet, emerald, crystal, ruby, lapis lazuli, diamonds, pearls with a white or pink cast

Shoes & handbags　Black, taupe, grey, burgundy, white. Burgundy works well with navy and black clothes

Hosiery　Neutral, taupe, beige, navy, grey, black

Dark-skinned brunettes

Hair colour:
Dark brown, brown-black, black. Hair is strong, healthy and coarse, with black highlights

Complexion:
Light brown, deep brown, rich mahogany, black, smooth and often velvety looking. It is sometimes uneven and blotchy in colour

Eye colour:
Hazel, dark brown, black, occasionally grey or grey-green

Long-stemmed white or red roses, geraniums and pink and purple orchids are a suitable setting for you. The dramatic palette of Picasso – basic black and white splashed with vivid shades of red, blue and violet – are the colours that flatter you. Your best colours are brilliant and intense – shocking pink, magenta, cobalt blue. For an elegant effect, wear shades of one neutral colour for a monochromatic look, choosing different textures of fabric. Soft pink and the palest of blue and lilac are also appealing. Warm colours are *not* for most women in this group – avoid olive, rust, gold and yellow-orange, unless you wish to achieve a jarring contrast by combining red and orange. However, if your skin tone is coppery coloured and your hair tends

to have red highlights, you can wear yellow, orange and warm brown.
● The lighter skin tones in this group look particularly good in cobalt blue, ruby, soft pinks and the palest yellow.
● Darker skin tones can carry the very bright colours, as well as pure white.

All about hair
Your hair tends to be strong and healthy-looking. However, it may also have a natural bend to it, resulting in a wiry look which may be difficult to control. This type of hair looks its best when cut short (close to the ear and nape of the neck) and shaped. If your hair doesn't have too tight a curl, it can be left long, either in its natural curl or perhaps straightened to make it easier to manage when you create different hair styles.

Tightly-plaited hairstyles or hair intertwined with false pieces look particularly good on you, as do turbans and headbands.

Your hair tends to have a silvery look when it greys. Should you prefer to cover the grey, keep to your natural colour, or to any soft browns. Avoid red or orange tones when colouring, as they do not flatter your complexion.

18 of 66

Dark-skinned brunette types

Black hair
Deep brown complexion
Dark brown eyes

Brown-black hair
Golden brown complexion
Deep brown eyes

Dark brown hair
Light brown complexion
Grey eyes

Brown hair
Dark mahogany complexion
Dark hazel eyes

Your colour chart

Generally, all brunettes can wear the same basic colours. However, brunettes with darker skins should go for the very bold colours (brilliant red, stark white, bright blue, hot pink) which will bring out the rich amber tones of your complexions.

The first ten colours are your core colours. Any one of these is appropriate for all the basic items in your wardrobe – coats, suits, skirts and trousers. The neutral shades are also the most suitable for accessories. The remaining colours are more adaptable as accent colours for smaller items such as sweaters, blouses and scarves.

On the following pages we recommend shades of these colours for choosing cosmetics, accessories and jewellery, and we suggest wardrobe colour combinations on p. 73.

You can carry your colours everywhere by taking your colour chart to use as a shopping guide.

Your core colours

YOUR NEUTRALS

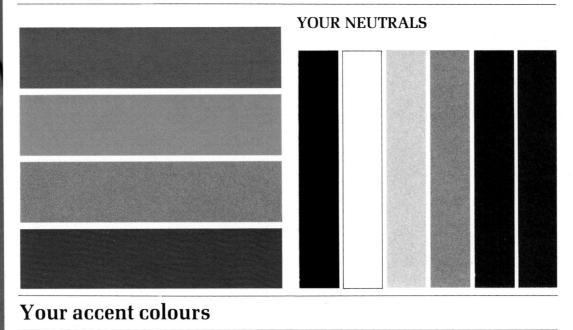

Your accent colours

Your best colours

Below are the right colours for your cosmetics and accessories. They reflect the colours we have set down for you on the previous page. Always think about the three or four colours in your wardrobe (see p. 73) and choose the "extras" to match them.

When you go shopping, take along your colour chart to help you choose a neutral handbag or a bright lipstick that will co-ordinate with your clothes. You will soon achieve a total look in which everything works together.

COSMETICS

Foundation   Amber, dark honey, copper-tan, beige-tan. Light or dark cover stick

Blusher   Bright red, plum, orchid, amber-rose, pink or red cheek gloss

Eye shadow   Shades of rose, plum, teal, mid-to-navy blue, smokey violet, taupe, blue-black

Eye liner   Electric blue, mauve, soft brown-black

Mascara   Brown-black, purple

Lipstick   Rose-red, brilliant red, plum, raspberry, mocha-red lipstick or gloss

Lip pencil   Plum, light brown

Nail varnish   Red, plum, fuchsia

ACCESSORIES

Glasses   If you wear glasses, you can wear more eye colour. Rose tones and smokey grey-violet eyeshadows create an attractive combination under clear-toned glasses. You can select thin red wire frames, grey, silver or clear frames

Jewellery   Diamanté in blue, pink or clear colours; ivory, onyx, garnet, sapphire, white pearls. Select rings, chains and earrings in silver or a combination of silver and gold

Shoes & handbags   Black and taupe; white and red for summer; silver for cocktail or evening wear

Hosiery   Slate grey, black, suntan shades; cobalt blue or red can be worn in thicker ribbed stockings

Colours in action

This woman's large round eyes are one of her best features. However, her patchy (light and dark) skin tone, high forehead and a bottom lip that is lighter in colour than the top all make her a prime candidate for a colour make-over.

Day

A dark concealer evens out her patchy skin and a bronze foundation gives all-over colour. Amber translucent powder makes the skin glow. Contouring in brown-toned blusher softens her square chin. A raspberry blusher on the cheekbones and temples and highlighter above the blusher (towards the hairline) create high cheekbones. Her eyes come to life with charcoal shadow on corners, brick on corners of brow bones and plum blended with charcoal on lids. A lip toner in her own lip colour matches bottom lip to top; plum lip pencil with light plum lipstick and a frosted gloss completes this sophisticated, professional look

Evening

An exciting party mood is achieved with vivid colour, shine and sparkle. Here a coppery tan foundation creates a richer, more shimmering look. Iridescent powder under the brow bone highlights and accents the eyes. Coal-black and midnight blue eye shadows are applied with a wet brush to outline the eyes and applied dry (and heavily) to the lids and corners and smudged. Both black and electric blue mascaras are stroked onto lashes to give them deep colour. Soft brown pencil outlines and shapes the lips and magenta frosted lipstick flashes colour. Fringe sprinkled with glitter will make her shimmer by night

This young woman, too, has problems common to many dark-skinned brunettes – her complexion is uneven, with dark tones around her nostrils and shadows under the eyes, and her bottom lip is lighter in colour than her top lip. Also, her hair is straggly and untidy; her heart-shaped face should be elongated by careful contouring.

Day

We applied concealer to block-out the shadows around her eyes, nostrils and laugh-lines. Copper and tan foundation colours are blended together to correct the uneven tone of her skin. Lip toner in a natural brown colour matches her bottom lip to her top lip; fuchsia lipstick is applied over this. Violet and mauve eye shadows blended on the lids, black kohl pencil and black mascara add depth to her captivating eyes. A mauve-pink blusher is placed in the middle of her high cheekbones, making the cheeks look more hollow, and above the temples and along the hairline, to make the widest part of her face appear more narrow

Evening

A copper glow foundation and pearlized, loose powder set her make-up. Tawny gold eye shadow is blended with plum towards the corner of the eyes and a beige highlighter applied to the brow bone. Soft blue-black pencil lines extend from the bottom lid towards the brow to create a winged look. Brown-black mascara is applied heavily, creating fuller lashes and emphasizing her almond-shaped eyes. Bright magenta-pink lipstick with a light glimmer of clear lip gloss on the bottom lip make her face sparkle. Pinky-red powder blush on the temples creates a soft effect and red cheek gloss adds a radiant glow to complete her evening look

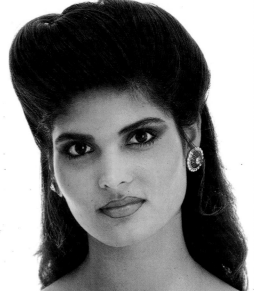

Pale blonde types

Flaxen hair
Pale, translucent complexion
Grey-blue eyes

Darkened blonde hair
Pinky-beige complexion
Teal blue eyes

Brown (once blonde) hair
Ruddy complexion
Light blue eyes

Your colour chart

The soft shades below are the ones that complement your delicate complexion.

The first ten colours are your core colours. Any one of these is appropriate for all the basic items in your wardrobe – coats, suits, skirts and trousers. The neutral shades are also the most suitable for accessories. The remaining colours are more adaptable as accent colours for smaller items such as sweaters, blouses and scarves.

On the following pages we recommend shades of these colours for choosing cosmetics, accessories and jewellery, and we suggest wardrobe colour combinations on p. 70.

You can carry your colours everywhere by taking your colour chart to use as a shopping guide.

Your core colours

YOUR NEUTRALS

Your accent colours

36

Golden blondes

Hair colour:
Light golden brown, Scandinavian blonde, strawberry blonde – all with natural golden tones

Complexion:
Peach or ivory; many have a tendency to blush easily

Eye colour:
Crystal blue, blue with brown flecks, blue-green or golden brown

Fields of cornflowers, daffodils and budding crocuses create the right background for the "golden girl". The palette of David Hockney, with its bright blues, golds, yellows and corals, is what flatters you most. Warm colours, that is, colours warmed with gold, are for you. Your best colours are the subtle shades of cream, ivory, peach and camel, the bright gold of the Californian sun and a clear Mediterranean blue. Ivory, cream, tan and soft brown blend beautifully with the golden shades of your hair, creating a monochromatic, all-in-one look which is chic and elegant.

● All golden blondes should avoid fuchsia, burgundy, magenta, white and dark grey. Black and pure white look good only on suntanned skin and could be eliminated from your wardrobe completely. Navy and cream are good colours to use as substitutes, especially for accessories.
● Golden blondes with peachy-beige complexions and blue eyes look particularly good in bright blue and coral tones.
● Ivory and ivory-peach complexions are enhanced by the softer shades of peach, sand and yellow-green.
● The darker golden blonde with more colour to her complexion is suited to golds and rusts, as well as the brighter corals and cornflower blues.

Altered hair colour
The combination of warm golden hair and a glowing complexion creates a bright, vivacious young look. But when your hair turns grey, consider dying it to its natural golden tone or golden brown. Or, leave your hair grey and highlight it with gold. Golden highlights can be very becoming on a light brown base, too.

Golden blonde types

Strawberry blonde hair
Pinky-peach complexion
Blue-green eyes

Tawny-gold hair
Creamy peach complexion
Turquoise-blue eyes

Darkened blonde hair
Golden-beige complexion
Hazel eyes

Your colour chart

The 24 shades below are best for the woman with the peaches-and-cream complexion.

The first ten colours are your core colours. Any one of these is appropriate for all the basic items in your wardrobe – coats, suits, skirts and trousers. The neutral shades are also the most suitable for accessories. The remaining colours are more adaptable as accent colours for smaller items such as sweaters, blouses and scarves.

On the following pages we recommend shades of these colours for choosing cosmetics, accessories and jewellery, and we suggest wardrobe colour combinations on p. 71.

You can carry your colours everywhere by taking your colour chart to use as a shopping guide.

Your core colours

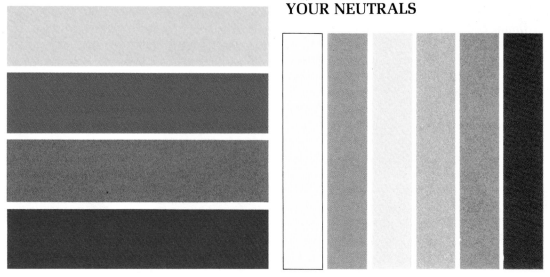

YOUR NEUTRALS

Your accent colours

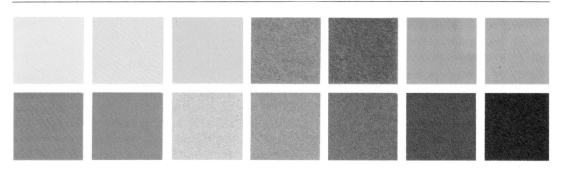

Redheads

Hair colour:
Light red to dark auburn, and brown hair with definite red or auburn highlights

Complexion:
Fair or reddish, copper-toned

Eye colour:
Turquoise, green or blue, golden brown

Vibrant flowers like tiger lilies, chrysanthymums and marigolds are those which best complement your exciting hair. Your best colours are those seen in paintings by Gauguin – lush greens, rich oranges, smudgy olives, terracotta. Redheads are fortunate because most designers use a wide selection of these colours, especially in the autumn.

Because your red hair is and should be the focus of attention, do not wear more than three colours at one time. One of the colours should blend with your hair: cinnamon, salmon or brick red. To achieve a more striking look, the second colour should be the colour of your eyes; if you have blue eyes use teal or aqua. A good three-colour combination for a brown-eyed auburn-redhead is brick red, cream and chocolate (for more combinations, see redhead wardrobe colours, p. 69). All redheads should avoid fuchsia, unless a harsh, brashy effect is desired. Pink, plum and black are not in the redhead's colour scheme at all.

● Redheads with fair or light, freckled pink complexions look best in softer shades – light beige, tan, salmon, olive and moss green – because very bright colours can be overwhelming.
● Redheads with copper skin look best in brighter colours, especially pumpkin, cinnamon-brown, brick, copper, topaz and bronze.
● Those light redheads whose hair colour is a cross between strawberry blonde and light carrot-red, and whose complexions are whitish-pink, can borrow some of the clearer colours of the golden blonde – coral, sand, aqua and Mediterranean blue.
● Brick red is an exciting colour for all redheads, and is very effective when combined with a neutral colour such as beige or bone.

Altered hair colour

Redheads do not grey attractively; the grey turns a tea colour and yellows with age. We recommend colouring the hair. Our rule for redheads is: as you grow older, go lighter.

If you use henna, use a red or gold shade, colours with warm tones. If you dye your hair, avoid any cool or ash tones. You are best in golden colours, from strawberry to golden blonde and auburn. Delicate gold highlights in red hair look attractive and natural, as if highlighted by the sun. Applying lowlights is particularly effective for auburn hair – that is, using a red colour just a shade or two lighter than your own. This results in a more subtle look than that of highlighting.

Redhead types

Brown hair (gold-red highlights)
Golden copper complexion
Green eyes

Dark auburn hair
Light peach complexion
Teal blue eyes

Auburn hair
Copper complexion
Topaz-coloured eyes

Dark carrot-red hair
Peach freckled complexion
Amber-coloured eyes

Your colour chart

Although your best colours are those of the autumn leaves – bright orange, brick red, ginger-brown – the 24 shades below will help you look great in any season.

The first ten colours are your core colours. Any one of these is appropriate for all the basic items in your wardrobe – coats, suits, skirts and trousers. The neutral shades are also the most suitable for accessories. The remaining colours are more adaptable as accent colours for smaller items such as sweaters, blouses and scarves.

On the following pages we recommend shades of these colours for choosing cosmetics, accessories and jewellery, and we suggest wardrobe colour combinations on p. 69.

You can carry your colours everywhere by taking your colour chart to use as a shopping guide.

Your core colours

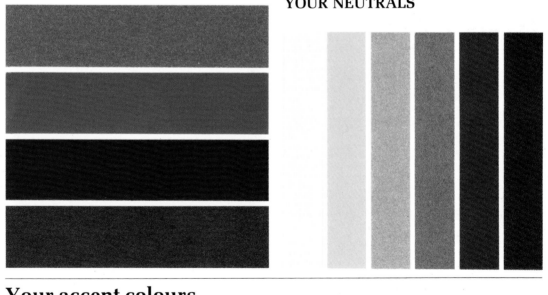

YOUR NEUTRALS

Your accent colours

Your best colours

Below are the right colours for your cosmetics and accessories. They reflect the colours we have set down for you on the previous page. Always think about the three or four colours in your wardrobe (see p. 69) and choose the "extras" to match them. When you go shopping, take along your colour chart to help you choose a neutral handbag or a bright lipstick that will co-ordinate with your clothes. You will soon achieve a total look in which everything – clothes, cosmetics and accessories – works together.

COSMETICS

Foundation   Golden beige, cream-beige, peach-beige

Blusher   Tawny, peach, apricot, coral

Eye shadow   Sludge green, russet, teal, golden copper

Eye liner   Moss green, charcoal, brown

Mascara   Dark brown, green

Lipstick   Brick red, coral, peach

Lip pencil   Light brown

Nail varnish   Coral, brick red

ACCESSORIES

Hosiery   Flesh tone, bone, tan, grey-beige, olive. Avoid pink

Shoes & handbags   Bone, tan, brown, olive

Glasses   If you wear glasses you can wear more eye colour. For green eyes, use teal and soft brown shadows; for golden brown eyes, ginger or copper; for brown eyes, teal or turquoise. If you wear tinted glasses, your lens colour should be in golden amber, peach or smokey brown tones. Tan, camel, russet-red or tortoise-shell frames suit you, as do gold, amber or skin-toned frames. Avoid pink, pale blue and red frames. Metal and clear plastic are not flattering either

Jewellery   Ivory, wood, coral, amber, tiger's eye, jade, turquoise, emerald, topaz, yellow diamonds, pearls with a yellow cast

Cosmetics

U se cosmetics to help you look and feel your best. Cosmetics enable you to emphasize your good features and to camouflage your flaws; they can provide a harmonious blend between your clothing and your hair. **Moisturizer** makes the skin feel soft and velvety and gives it a dewy look. It also helps foundation go on evenly and smoothly. For dry skin use more moisturizer; for oily skin less.

Primer is a cream or liquid used under foundation to eliminate any redness or yellowness in the complexion and create an even tone. It comes in shades of green, purple and apricot. Apply green if your complexion is red and blotchy, or purple if your skin is sallow. Apricot primer should be used on extremely pale or grey skin tones. It is also effective for black skin, as it "warms" the skin, giving it a bright glowing effect.

Foundation improves the skin's texture, covers small blemishes, gives an even-toned finish and provides protection against the environment. Choose a foundation colour as close to your skin colour as possible.

Concealers are effective in obliterating small blemishes and skin discolourations. They usually come in lipstick-type dispensers. Use a concealer to cover imperfections or to "light out" shadows under the eyes and around the nose, or lines at the side of the mouth. A concealer should not be more than two shades lighter than your skin, and should be subtly blended so that it is not obvious.

Powder sets the foundation and keeps it fresh-looking longer. If you use an oil-based foundation, powder prevents it from streaking. If you have oily skin, powder removes the shine. Powders

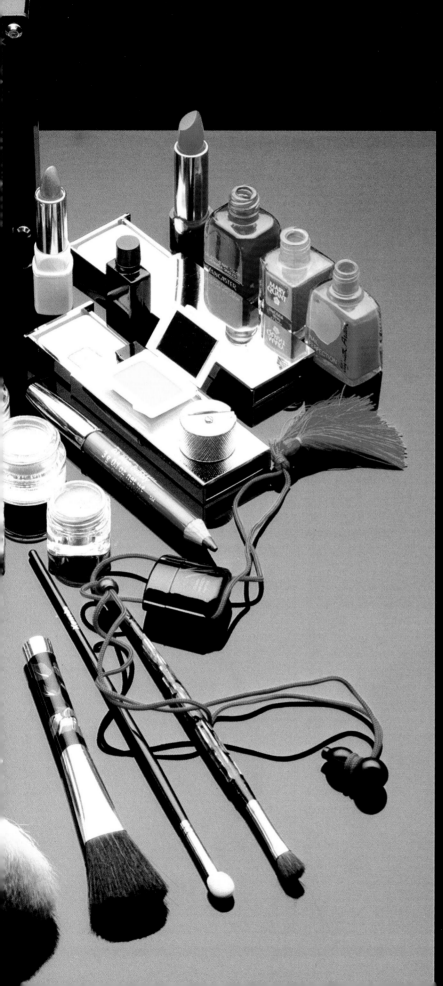

come in various shades, so choose one that matches your skin type. Translucent powder can be used for all types of skin; it has no colour and will not change the shade of the foundation. To give an all-over luminous look, use iridescent or pearlized powder.

Blusher, or rouge, comes in powder, cream or liquid form and is applied with a brush, a damp sponge or your fingertips. It should harmonize with your lipstick colour and skin toner. The lighter your skin, the lighter your blusher should be.

Eyebrow pencils can help you create a more expressive face, as you use them to reshape your eyebrows. You will need two pencils, one in your natural hair colour and the other a shade lighter for highlighting. The combination of these colours will give a more natural look.

Eye shadow comes in several forms: pressed powder, loose powder, cream stick and liquid cream. Choose whichever you are most comfortable with. The colour needn't match your eye tone, but make sure that it does not overpower your natural eye colour.

Eye liner makes the lashes appear fuller, but it should be applied subtly. Use either a pencil or a fine-tipped sable brush. Neutral smoky shades such as charcoal, grey and brown give the most natural look.

Mascara accentuates the eyes and gives them depth and dimension. It comes in cake or cream form and can be applied with brushes, wands or combs.

Lipstick comes in sticks, creams, and glosses, as tubes or in pots. Outlining your lips with a lip brush or pencil will help you follow your natural lip line smoothly and accurately and results in a clean, neat look.

Hair

Beauty begins with the hair. If your hair doesn't look right, your total look will be wrong. To look its best, your hair must be clean. Frequent shampooing is not damaging to the hair, provided you choose a shampoo that is specially formulated for your hair type.

Shampoos

Shampoo for normal hair will clean hair without drying it. Shampoo for oily hair will remove excess oil. Shampoo for damaged hair is extra-gentle. When you shampoo, work suds into the scalp first, then through your hair, massaging gently with your fingertips (not nails). A lot of lather is not necessary; neither is more than one washing unless you have very oily hair. Use warm, not hot, water and rinse well. A final rinse with cool water gives the hair more shine.

Conditioners

Conditioners work wonders for the hair. They prevent and repair damage to the hair, add body to thin hair and make hair easier to comb and style. Conditioners are applied after shampooing and rinsing. Remember that they are formulated for the hair, not the scalp, and work best on the ends.

There are two types of conditioners: instant conditioners which are left on the hair for a few minutes, and penetrating conditioners which remain on the hair for 15–30 minutes. The penetrating conditioners work best for "problem" hair.

Damaged hair

Excessive heat from hair dryers, electric rollers or curling irons and chemically-induced changes to the hair such as colouring, straightening or permanent waves, may cause breaking, split ends, and dryness. But don't despair if your hair is damaged – there are several things you can do to revitalize it:

● Cut the split ends often, and get a style that requires as little setting as possible. Try to let your hair dry naturally.

● Massage your scalp gently to stimulate the oil glands.

● Use a hot oil treatment or a penetrating conditioner every two weeks.

● Use a wide-toothed comb and a soft-bristled brush.

● To give your hair a shinier, healthier look, use a cream "thickener" and let it remain on your hair between shampoos. Thickeners contain proteins and oils that coat the hair with an invisible film, making the hair thicker and giving the illusion of more volume. For best results, it should be applied after every shampoo.

Colouring your hair

The key to choosing the right hair colour is knowing what is harmonious with your natural colouring. Redheads look most effective when warm golden glints or red tones are added to their hair. Most blondes look attractive with subtle highlights, which can give them a chic, expensive look. Medium-to-dark brown hair colour is most suitable for olive, sallow, ruddy-skinned or dark-skinned brunettes; warm red tones are not. Brunettes with fair or white complexions should choose ash-brown, dark brown or brown-black shades. Those determined to go blonde should consider beige-blonde or ash-blonde highlights framing the face rather than an all-over colour. This creates a softer, younger-looking effect.

Changing your hair colour can make a dramatic change in your looks. For the best results go to a professional. We recommend that the permanent colourings – highlighting and lowlighting, tinting and bleaching – be applied only by a hairdresser. However, the hair colouring products which are often used at home with little difficulty are: shampoo and henna rinses, coloured gels and mousses. Always test a home colouring product for allergic reaction before using it on your entire head and read all the instructions carefully.

Shampoo rinses are left on the hair after regular shampooing, then rinsed out. Depending on the product, this temporary colour can last anywhere between one and six shampoos.

Gels and mousses are used for styling and conditioning, as well as temporary colouring. They can be massaged into wet or dry hair and either finger-dried or blow-dried. Both gels and mousses add a subtle all-over colour to the hair.

Henna is a natural dye which is mainly used to give an all-over reddish tint. It comes as a powder, which is mixed with hot water to form a paste and applied to damp hair. Being a natural colouring, henna does not damage hair. However, it should not be used on fair hair or grey hair, as it may result in a bright orange colour.

Highlighting is applying permanent dye to selected strands of hair, giving a soft effect of added colour. A perforated rubber cap is placed tightly on the head and fine strands are pulled through the holes. A colour solution is then applied to the strands. Some salons add highlights by sectioning strands separately from the rest of the hair and wrapping them in silver foil, leaving them until the desired colour is reached.

Lowlighting is a very subtle way of brightening the hair. Shades of the same colour are subtly blended to add rich colour tones to your natural hair colour. It is usually applied to brown hair to give reddish-brown lights.

Tinting makes the original hair colour lighter or darker by up to four shades. It can be very effective on all types of hair and is often used to cover grey.

Bleaching is a strong permanent chemical method – it can make hair as light as you want. A paste is painted onto the roots and through the ends of the hair. Bleach contains both ammonia and peroxide, which are damaging to the hair, so deep conditioning treatments (the best are given by professionals) should be used to keep hair healthy.

HAIR STYLES
The right colour, the right cut, the right styling – these are the elements for making the most of your hair.

Just as cosmetics are effective in changing the shape of your face, so are different hair styles.

To change the look of a square face, you need to draw attention away from the jaw. Get plenty of fullness on top of your head – wearing hair off the forehead elongates the face, and wisps of hair near the jawbone softens the harsh square look.

If you have a round face, cutting your hair close to the nape of your neck makes your neck, and consequently your face, appear longer; more volume on top also lengthens the face and an asymmetrical fringe creates a narrowing illusion. Short, blunt-cut hair sweeping upwards draws the eye "up" and adds length to a round face.

The temples and forehead of a heart-shaped face benefit by the softening effect brought on by short hair which is brushed back into a sleek wave. The layered bob "cuts" into the widest part of the jaw, giving a narrower appearance.

A long face needs a lot of fullness on the sides for balance, especially if the chin is rather narrow, like our model's. A thick headband flattens the crown of the head and shortens the face.

Square Face

Round Face

Heart-shaped Face

Long Face

61

Figure types

The advertising media have created an ideal woman – she has perfect proportions and a complete lack of figure faults. She is usually five or six inches taller than the average woman, and much slimmer.

Few of us fall into this perfect mould – short women want to look tall, overweight women want to look slim, the tall want to lead attention away from their height and thin women strive for a more rounded look.

The following pages illustrate the difference which the right or wrong selection of clothing can make for imperfect figure shapes.

SHORT – WRONG

Padded shoulders and wide lapels accentuate angular cut of suit and create horizontal lines

Wide sleeves make arms look shorter

Jacket too long for this skirt length

Gathered skirt adds fullness and width

Dark suit and light stockings "cut" legs, creating a squat look

SHORT – RIGHT

Soft design of shoulders and overblouse creates more fluid lines

Diagonal line across bodice lengthens torso

One-piece, straight-cut dress with slight diagonal at hem elongates the body

Stockings and shoes in same colour accentuate vertical line

SHORT

Small women seem to shrink in large prints, horizontal stripes, outfits with wide belts and shirts with large cuffs. However, they can walk tall in vertical stripes, one-piece jumpsuits, wrap-around dresses and short jackets.

TALL

Tall women should avoid tiny prints, three-quarter sleeves, tiny earrings and dainty jewellery. They can minimize their height by wearing large coats, sweeping capes and pleated trousers or trousers with wide legs.

TALL – WRONG

TALL – RIGHT

Dark blouse with high neck makes neck appear longer

High-cut shoulders make arms appear longer

Blouse gives a short-waisted, long-legged look

Vertical stripes elongate the body

Long skirt adds height to body

Stockings in same colour as shoes create long-legged look

Layered clothes (light-coloured blouse, scarf and jacket with wide lapels) add breadth

Full sleeves with cuffs "shorten" arms

Wide belt divides body into more equal proportions

Tucks in skirt add fullness

Skirt just below knees "cuts" long legs

Light-coloured stockings break monotony and long vertical line of body

HEAVY FIGURE

The heavy-set woman seems to put on weight by wearing clothes with horizontal stripes or large designs, gathered skirts, skirts or dresses with patch pockets at the hips, clinging fabrics, and bulky long-haired furs. She can look slimmer by choosing vertical stripes and patterns, V-neck sweaters, skirts that have a central inverted pleat, outfits in one colour only (including hose and shoes) and dress lengths below the knee.

HEAVY – WRONG

Wide cross-collar accentuates a thick neck

Wide cut of bodice adds fullness to waist and hips

Large plaid design creates horizontal line, adding width to body

Shoes with ankle straps make legs look shorter

HEAVY – RIGHT

Detail on shoulder brings the eye "up", creating a longer line

Soft, draping effect of diagonal over-blouse is more flattering

Solid-coloured dress is more slenderizing

Longer dress length adds to height and creates a slimmer look

THIN FIGURE

The very thin woman shouldn't wear sleeveless dresses, fabrics with small prints or two-piece dresses (dresses with short jackets). She'll fill out nicely in clothes with horizontal stripes, plaids and patterns; double-breasted suit jackets; skirts with large patch pockets; pleated trousers; blouses with yokes, ruffles and gathers and patterned or textured hose in light colours worn with simple, stylish shoes.

THIN – WRONG

Shoulders are "sharp" and shapeless

V-neckline adds length to thin neck

Clinging jersey fabric emphasizes thin shape

Dark, straight dress elongates the body

Below-knee dress length gives "leggy" look

Dark stockings accentuate skinny legs

Thick-soled shoes contrast delicate legs

THIN – RIGHT

Big white collar and puff shoulders of textured sweater give wider look

Light colours give larger, but softer effect

Very full culottes add width

Longer skirt gives legs "shorter" look

Light-coloured stockings add fullness

Thin flat heels don't overpower slender legs

65

Clothes

The way you dress gives people an immediate impression of who you are. Research studies have shown that well-dressed people are judged to be more qualified, more intelligent and more likeable than those who are not. They are treated with respect and are given greater social and business opportunities.

Your appearance can also be the expression of a specific image you want to convey. The right clothes can project an artistic, provocative, authoritative, or demure image; the wrong clothes may indicate neglect, carelessness, or an unawareness of what is appropriate for a certain occasion.

Look through your wardrobe and decide whether or not your clothes reflect the image you want to project. Do they suit your way of life? Do they bring out your most flattering self? If the answer is "no", don't panic! You needn't change your entire wardrobe. Careful planning can result in a wardrobe full of clothes that are functional, versatile and lasting, without resulting in an empty purse.

Selecting colours

We'd like to help you create a wardrobe that is both effective and efficient. The first and easiest method is to choose three colours that go together well. Find your colour group in the following pages and note the suggested three-colour combinations. Choose one of the combinations and select individual articles of clothing in these colours only. Of course, if you prefer, add a fourth colour that goes well with the rest. However, it is not practical to have more than four colours in your wardrobe unless many items are in the "neutral" shades.

Another way to build an effective wardrobe is to start with a neutral colour, then add two or three other colours that work well together. For example, taupe works well with purple or black; grey with burgundy and navy. Wardrobe consultants choose one medium-to-dark colour and use this for the nucleus, or core, of a client's wardrobe in items like coats, jackets and trousers. These clothes are more versatile in solid colours rather than prints. Other shades – accent colours – are added through smaller items such as sweaters, blouses and scarves.

Choosing clothes

The next step is co-ordinating separates. Treat each article of clothing as a separate unit. When you buy a suit, consider it as two separate pieces of clothing, a skirt and a jacket, each of which can be worn with other items. Therefore, the jacket can serve as a blazer worn with your other skirts and trousers or over a dress. Choose simple, classic styles with a minimum of detail, as they can be easily interchanged with your other separates.

The third step to a successful wardrobe is choosing clothes for their versatility. Buy clothing that can be worn for several occasions. For example, a shirtwaist dress combined with a blazer can be worn during the day. For evening, try the same dress without the blazer, open the neck to reveal a lacy camisole top and wear high heeled shoes and dressy jewellery.

A suit is very dependable, as it can be worn for many occasions. Light-coloured suits require a darker blouse for businesswear; a light-coloured blouse looks elegant. The dark suit (navy or black) looks more serious and authoritative than a light one, and is more flexible, as it can be worn for both day and evening. For work, choose a classic white shirt; for evening or theatre, a silk shirt, pearl necklace and other dressy jewellery.

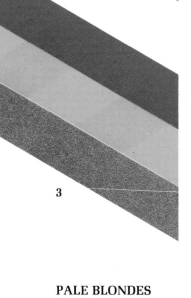

1

2

3

PALE BLONDES
Blondes should think
"soft and subtle"
when co-ordinating
ensembles. Pale
blondes can dream up
a wardrobe based on
colours such as
mushroom, pink,
camel and sand.

1

2

3

GOLDEN BLONDES
Golden blondes
should substitute
peach or coral for
pink. Natural fabrics
– lightweight wools,
gaberdines, knits,
silks and linens – feel
delightful and look
great in soft colours.

Suggested
3-colour
combinations

1

2

3

BRUNETTES
Dramatic contrasts of
light and dark set the
stage for a basic
brunette wardrobe.
Make your debut in
black, white, red and
grey, a combination
that's easy to achieve
and always glamor-
ous to wear.

1

2

3

**DARK-SKINNED
BRUNETTES**
Your other three-
colour combinations
are found above, but
you're certain to steal
the show in black,
red and purple.
Flannels, crisp
cottons, fine wools,
silks and satins are
your fabrics.

73

The look:
Efficient, energetic, imaginative

Hair:
A good cut that's easy to manage

Wardrobe:
Mainly mix-and-match separates – skirts, sweaters and blouses. For a practical look, wear monochromatic schemes with clothes in different textures

Cosmetics:
Shouldn't be too harsh or too heavy. Bright-coloured lipstick shouldn't be applied too thickly. Eye shadows should be well-blended, and eye liner not too severe

Jewellery
Simple watch, rings, and necklaces. Costume jewellery is fine, but keep it small

Fragrance:
Flowery scents – sandalwood, orange blossom and lilac

What to avoid:
Too many colours in one outfit – three co-ordinating colours in clothing and accessories should be the limit. Also avoid sparkling jewellery, outlandish hairstyles, and gold and glittery eye and lip make-up

Tips:
Solid-coloured blouses, especially light colours rather than prints, provide more versatility

The look:
Elegant, expensive, impeccable

Hair:
Neat, controlled, chic

Wardrobe:
High quality, understated clothes in natural fabrics (linen, silk, cotton, wool, cashmere). Monochromatic colour schemes or dark solids with colour accents in scarves or blouses. Wardrobe includes: suits, cashmere twin sets, cardigans, silk shirts.

Cosmetics:
Conservative, never obvious. Cosmetics include sheer foundation, translucent powder, eyeshadows in muted colours

Jewellery:
Pearls, chain necklaces, antique jewellery, modern gold or silver pieces

Fragrance:
Fresh scents like lavender and orchid; musk for evening

What to avoid:
Costume jewellery, see-through fabrics, off-the-shoulder blouses or sweaters, gimmicky or novelty type clothes

Tips:
Invest in accessories like designers' scarves or shoes. Try the menswear department for silk scarves to wear under coats or suits

THE AFTER FIVE LOOK

The look:
Smooth and
sophisticated

Hair:
Tousled or sleek, but
well-styled.

Cosmetics:
Heavier eye make-up
than for daytime, but
subtly blended, with
graduated colours
(pink, purple and
violet, for example)
and glistening high-
lighter in silver, gold
or peachy-pin;
lipstick should be a
shade darker than
day-time colour

Wardrobe:
Skirts in silk, taffeta,
or crepe with match-
ing or contrasting
blouses in silk or
satin; velvet or
brocaded jackets;
dresses in brocade or
silk

Jewellery:
Three-stranded pearl
choker with cameo
or diamanté clasps;
heavy chain necklace
with a big artificial or
real diamond
pendant; diamond
studded earrings,
emeralds, rubies,
sapphires

Fragrance:
Spicy scents
(cinnamon, ginger,
clove) or oriental
blends (musk, civet)
in heady, lingering
aromas

What to avoid:
Too much jewellery or
lots of different-
coloured stones in
one piece

Tips:
Invest in an expensive
evening bag and
wrap, like a velvet
cape

THE AGE OF EXPERIENCE

The look:
Graceful, dignified, personable

Hair:
Soft-looking, swept off the face, never longer than shoulder-length

Cosmetics:
Sheer foundation; softer lipstick and blusher colours; avoid harsh or silvery colours on eyes

Wardrobe:
Tailored, classic styles; unmatched suits, short-style jackets and blouses with slightly-puffed sleeves that give a youthful look

Jewellery
Bulky or geometric-shaped earrings can improve the less-than-perfect jawline. Pearls and beads inter-wined create a luxurious look

Fragrance:
Fresh floral scents (rose, gardenia, jasmine) and fruity scents (lemon, lime)

What to avoid:
Dull mousy colours, long dangling ear-rings which tend to pull the face down-ward, very blue or purple lipstick. Don't wait too long to re-touch colour if you have coloured your grey hair

Tips:
Wear soft fabrics in unconstructed jackets, and soft, crushy belts; wear collars open. Pay attention to your posture and grooming to retain a young attitude

The new you

Maybe you don't have the ideal figure or the perfect proportions to make you look great in absolutely anything you wear, or maybe you're tired of the same style clothes or hairdo you've worn for the past four or five years. Perhaps you want to change your image and let the world see a new side to your personality. Anything is possible if you choose your clothes and cosmetics carefully, select a becoming hairstyle and wear a smile!

This busy mother of five has a part-time job in the evenings. She has little time to devote to applying cosmetics or shopping for clothes. She is 5′ 7″ tall and wears a size 16 dress.

We have chosen a very practical suit for her in hard-wearing corduroy. A shocking pink blouse and scarf provide a wonderful accent to her attractive dark colouring. Her eyes were coloured with soft pink and violet eye shadows, and her lipstick and blusher are in fuchsia tones. Her hair was permed and restyled into an easy-to-manage bob.

This woman in her
early twenties has
outgrown her trendy
teen look. She has
little idea of how to
dress for the more
professional working
world she plans to
enter. While she is of
average height (5′ 6″)
and dress size (12),
and has no particular
figure faults, her
image can be
changed completely
with the help of the
right clothes and
cosmetics.

In keeping with her
casual style, we chose
a fawn trouser suit
with toning checked
shirt. High brown
boots and matching
scarf complete this
slightly "mannish"
look, which is
softened by a bow at
the neck, but little
jewellery. Her hair is
trim and neat, and
make-up shades of
beige and brown
maintain a natural
look.

This young grand-
mother has not really
changed her image
since she was a
"hippy" in the 1960s.
Today her look is
neither fashionable
nor flattering. She is
4′ 11″ tall, wears a
large dress size, and
is short-waisted.

She looks taller
and slimmer in her
pleated camel skirt
and long waistcoat,
which camouflage
her short waist and
slims her hips. The
checked scarf also
draws the eye down-
ward creating the
illusion of height
which is so important
for petite women;
and worn with its
matching hat, makes
a smart finish to this
classic ensemble.
Her hair has been
cut shorter and swept
off her face to give
a more youthful
appearance. A warm
peach foundation,
coral lipstick and
teal blue eye shadow
all contribute to her
new, more contem-
porary look.

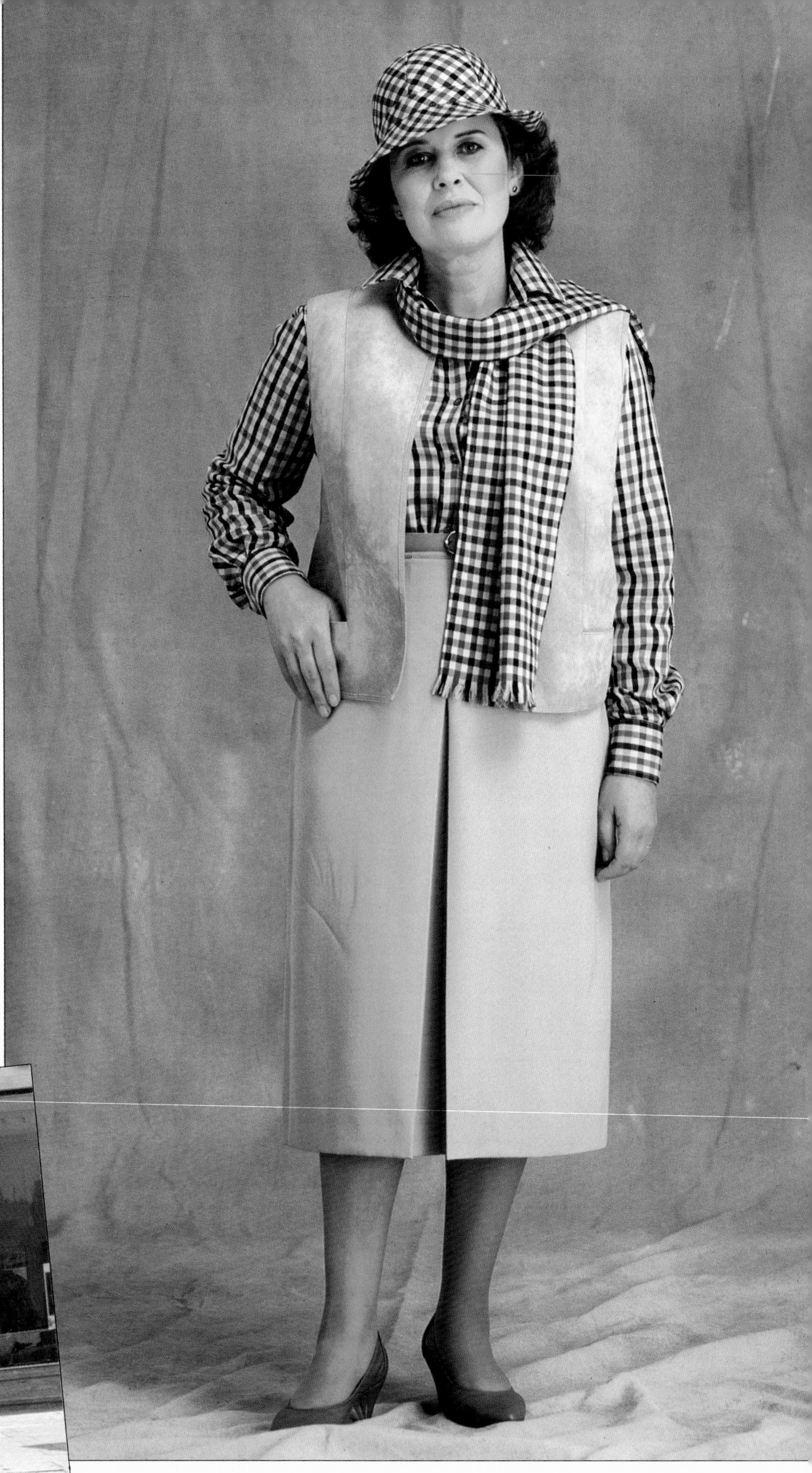

This older, petite woman, just under 5 foot, is overweight (wears a size 20 dress) and has a large bust. She also has a full face with a double chin and wears little make-up.

A crepe dress with box pleats was chosen for her as it creates a long line, thus adding height to her figure. Long strands of pearls echo the vertical line; a matching hat adds softness and elegance.

Her hair was lightened to an ash grey-blonde and styled off her face in an "upswept" wave. Cosmetics were applied subtly – concealer under the eyes eliminates puffiness; contouring with rose-brown blush reshapes her full cheeks; teal blue eye colour and pink-mauve lipstick and blusher contribute to the overall softness of her new face.

Travel

Travelling can be a nightmare if you are over-burdened with heavy suit-cases. However, with your new colour and clothes know-how, you can travel with the minimum of luggage and the maximum of changes.

Choose two co-ordinating colours from your scheme (or several shades of one colour) and select clothes in these colours that are both practical and versatile. If you are a brunette, we recommend either a black-and-red or a taupe-and-purple colour combination. A pale blonde might like french blue and burgundy or ice pink and off-white with the colour accent in a navy scarf. Golden blondes look nice in camel and grey or Mediterranean blue and daffodil yellow. Cinnamon and dark chocolate or brick red and cream are winning combinations for the travelling redhead.

By mixing and matching individual articles, you can create a wardrobe with enough variety to last your entire trip, be it three days or three weeks. Below are suggestions for the minimum number of clothes to take on two city trips – one is for five days, the other for four weeks.

The woman on the facing page is taking a four-week trip. Overleaf are twelve additional outfits that she can put together with our simple formula.

What to pack for a five-day city trip:

1 suit
1 skirt
1 pr. trousers
2 blouses (1 day, 1 evening)
1 sweater
1 scarf
1 coat
hat (optional)
2 prs. shoes
2 handbags (1 day, 1 evening)
1 nightdress, dressing gown, folding
  slippers
3 prs. tights
3 sets underwear
1 slip
jewellery

What to pack for a four-week city trip:

2 suits
1 skirt
2 prs. trousers
5 blouses (3 day, 2 evening)
3 sweaters (1 cardigan, 2 pullovers)
1 waistcoat
2 scarves
1 coat
hat (optional)
2 prs. shoes
2 handbags (1 day, 1 evening)
2 nightdresses, dressing gown, folding
  slippers
5 prs. tights
5 sets underwear
1 slip
jewellery

Note: Don't forget your cosmetic bag and hair-dryer!

Stepping out Ten o'clock meeting, luncheon at one, three o'clock appointment, drinks at five, dinner at eight, dancing 'til ? ... Whatever the schedule or the occasion, the fashion-conscious woman will travel right – and light – by colour-co-ordinating her clothes and packing the most versatile items. More than

thirty changes of clothes are possible in our four-week trip, twelve of which are shown above.
The two suits are in light and dark shades of one colour, but they needn't be – just pick colours that will match everything else. With a different look every day, you'll never be bored with your clothes!

Acknowledgements

Dorling Kindersley would like to thank the following people for their help in producing this book:

Illustrators
Shari Peacock, Lynne Robinson

Photography for cover and page 56
Colin Thomas

Stylist
Liz E. London

Make-up Artists
Peter Coburn, Keiko Eno, Audrey Maxwell, Miguel Mendoza, Helen Robertson

Hair Stylists
Gregory Cazaly and Paula Mann from Joshua Galvin Hair Salon, Margaret Friel from Trevor Sorbie

Reproduction
Reprocolor International

Typesetters
Chambers Wallace

Elizabeth Arden

to whom we are extremely grateful for their extensive help in providing cosmetics, which were used throughout the book

ANGLIA TELEVISION
who kindly gave permission to reproduce the "before" pictures (pages 88, 90 and 91) from their ABOUT ANGLIA feature "The New You"

Alexon, Aquascutum of London Limited, Castleberry Knits, Dickins and Jones, Fenn Wright and Manson Ltd., Harrods, Hobbs, I Blues, Shoes by Charles Jourdan, Soo Yung Lee, Lumiere, Adrien Mann Jewellery, Mansfield Originals Ltd., Next, Harvey Nichols, Albert Nipon, Ports of Bond Street International Ltd., Selfridges, Miss Selfridge, David Shilling (hats on pp. 40 and 77), Gianni Versace, Viva, Wallis, Fashion Fair Beauty Products and Kanebo Cosmetics